THE BEST EVER
BRIEF HISTORY OF THE
New York Yankees

BY
DAVE McGRAIL

To Leila, Cassie, Joey, Molly, Ryan,
Leighton, Makena, Dash, and Callahan.
And to Don Mattingly. And not to Wade Boggs.

TABLE OF CONTENTS

ACKNOWLEDGMENTS

My deepest gratitude to my fantastic editor, good friend, and partner-in-crime on various projects, Catherine Milligan.

Special thanks to the kids who read and commented on the many drafts of the book. If you want a brutally honest opinion, just ask an eight-year-old.

A BRIEF HISTORY OF NEW YORK CITY

*N*ew York City is not the capital of New York State (do you know what is?), but it is the largest city in the United States, with over 8 million people residing there. There's a lot of business in New York City, almost as much as there is in the entire *country* of Canada. One difference, however, is that you can ice fish in Canada, while you can't ice fish on Wall Street in New York City. Trust me, don't even try it—the experiment might seem funny, but not to the police officers who come to break it up, and then you'll have to explain to them that you are doing research for a book about the New York Yankees, which doesn't really sound believable.

New York City didn't always have 8 million people. For thousands of years, the land was inhabited by

Native American tribes. Then, Dutch settlers (from the Netherlands, in Europe), came to town in the 1600s to spread joy. Sorry, no, not joy; disease. They came to spread disease.

The British took over the city in 1664 and changed the name to "New York" after the Duke of York. It's a good thing they didn't name the city after the Earl of Sandwich, right? Otherwise, this book would be about the New Sandwich Yankees.

The British chased George Washington out of New York in 1776 during the Revolutionary War. But Washington was one tough dude, and he returned in 1783, when the colonies won their independence from Britain.

During the 1800s, many immigrants flocked to New York City and, beginning in 1886, they were greeted by the Statue of Liberty, a gift from France.

During the 1900s, New York City became home to the Empire State Building (1931), the World's Fair (1939 and 1964), and the United Nations (1952). It also became home to something else monumental. Can you guess what that is? I'll give you a hint—it's a baseball team whose name rhymes with "hankies."

WHAT IS A "YANKEE"?

*T*he definition of Yankee depends on whom you ask. Urbandictionary.com provides this wonderful description:

- To foreigners, a Yankee is an American.
- To Americans, a Yankee is a Northerner.
- To Easterners, a Yankee is a New Englander.
- To New Englanders, a Yankee is a Vermonter.
- And in Vermont, a Yankee is somebody who eats pie for breakfast.

I grew up in Connecticut, which is in New England. I have never had pie for breakfast, but I once had quiche, which is sort of like pie. Am I a "Yankee"? Who knows?

Anyway, because New York's team was in the American League, it was called the "New York Americans." In 1904, a sports writer started referring to the team as the Yankees (or "Yanks"). The name stuck, just like spaghetti when you throw it at a wall. No, I mean *cooked* spaghetti, ya goofball!

The New York Yankees have been wearing pinstripes for a hundred years. Rumor has it that the Yankees started wearing pinstripes to help Babe Ruth look slimmer. If that's true, then over the years some other Yankees might have benefited from this decision as well:

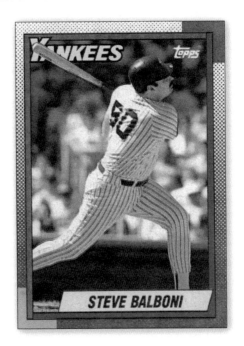

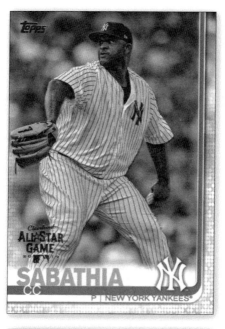

YANKEES OVER
THE YEARS

$\mathcal{T}$he Yankees have won 27 World Series, more than any other team in the history of Major League Baseball! In fact, they have won more titles than any team in the NBA, NFL, or NHL.

The Yankees seized their first World Series in 1923. Babe Ruth batted .393 that year and .368 in the World Series. Ruth loved being a Yankee, being in the spotlight, having fun, and joking around with kids. He retired with a .342 batting average, 714 career home runs, and—get this—94 wins *as a pitcher*.

After the 1923 victory, the Yankees also won the World Series in 1927, 1928, 1932, 1936, 1937, 1938, 1939, 1941, 1943, 1947, 1949, 1950, 1951, 1952, 1953, 1956, 1958, 1961, 1962, 1977, 1978, 1996, 1998, 1999, 2000, and 2009.

The team that triumphed from 1936 through 1939 featured Lefty Gomez, who had a 6-0 record in the World Series, and Joe DiMaggio, who still holds the record for the longest hitting streak (56 games) and, in case you were wondering, for the shortest marriage to Marilyn Monroe (just over a year).

Winning teams in the 1950s starred Mickey Mantle, Whitey Ford, and Yogi Berra; in the 1970s, the Yankees won with Reggie Jackson, who hit three home runs in Game 6 of the 1977 World Series; and in the 1990s and 2000s, they grabbed more titles with Mariano Rivera, Derek Jeter, and Jorge Posada.

You will note that the Yankees did not win a World Series during the 1980s. Sadly, that was the decade when I was a kid, devoted to watching or listening to every single Yankees game religiously. More about this later.

In the next few pages, you will learn about six particularly great Yankees. Perhaps you'll be surprised, and maybe some adults will even be outraged, that these pages do not spotlight Mickey Mantle, Reggie Jackson, Billy Martin, Roger Clemons, Alex Rodriguez, Roger Maris, Thurman Munson,

Rich "Goose" Gossage, Catfish Hunter, Andy Pettitte, Bernie Williams, Aaron Boone, or others.

To those miffed adults, I say: let's keep in mind that the title of this book is "The Best Ever *Brief* History ..." Also, not every Yankee was a perfect role model (I'm looking at you, Mantle and Clemons), and, parents, you are in a much better position than I to discuss the inevitable Munson follow-up questions with your kids.

And to any readers who are still puzzling over the list above, yes, the Yankees not only had a "Lefty" and a "Whitey," but also a "Catfish" and a "Goose." Go figure!

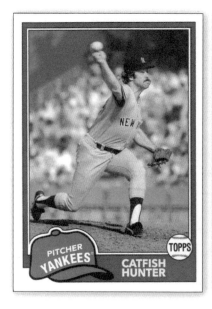

LOU GEHRIG

*L*ou Gehrig played seventeen seasons for the New York Yankees, from 1923-1939. He had a career .340 batting average, .632 slugging percentage, and .447 on base percentage. He also hit 493 home runs and had 1,995 RBIs. With these stats, it is no surprise the Gehrig is widely regarded as one of the best players of all time.

Gehrig played in 2,130 consecutive games, a record that was not broken until 1995 (when Cal Ripken surpassed this streak, going on to play in 2,632 straight games). Gehrig still holds the American League record for most RBIs in a season—184 in 1931—and he was the first American League player to hit four home runs in a game.

In 1934, Gehrig won the Triple Crown. This fact may be a bit confusing for some, because the Triple Crown title also applies to horse racing. It is awarded to the three-year-old Thoroughbred horse that wins the Kentucky Derby, Preakness Stakes, and Belmont Stakes. Also, Gehrig was nicknamed the "Iron Horse." Did he race against horses when he wasn't playing first base for the Yankees? It's unlikely. Horses, I bet, would find it downright insulting to be challenged to a race by a human, even Lou Gehrig. But I digress.

In any event, Gehrig won the Triple Crown in 1934 with an incredible .363 batting average, 49 home runs, and 166 RBIs.

Lou Gehrig was also a really good guy. He embodied professionalism, modesty, and grit. You'd probably enjoy having an apple juice with him. Tragically, he had a debilitating disease, now called "Lou Gehrig's disease," and had to retire from baseball at age 36. Two years later he gave an incredible farewell speech at Yankee Stadium, often referred to as the "Luckiest Man on the Face of the Earth" speech. If you watch it with an adult who loves baseball, you might get to see them cry.

A Lou Gehrig baseball card from the 1920s or 1930s is really expensive, and as a writer and part-time philosopher, I am not in a position to afford one. I do, however, have this 2012 "tribute card" which I bought online for three bucks when I was shopping for some new socks and a pair of earbuds to replace the ones I sat on and broke.

YOGI BERRA

*L*awrence "Yogi" Berra played for the Yankees from 1946-63 and then managed them in 1964. He was an 18-time All-Star and three-time American League MVP, capturing *ten* World Series championships. That's an MLB record. In short, Berra was a winner.

Strangely, Yogi Berra's reputation as a baseball star might be rivaled by his fame in another category—one that nobody really strives to dominate. Have you ever heard of "malapropisms"? A malapropism is a sort of language accident: it's the misuse or mix-up of words or phrases, often resulting in a funny or ridiculous statement. If you're not sure how to say the word itself, give it a few more tries... and then don't worry about it for now—I still can't pronounce it either!

Berra was the king of malapropisms. Reporters loved him because he not only gave them great sports to write about but also great quotes. Here are some of Berra's most famous sayings:

1. When you come to a fork in the road, take it.
2. You can observe a lot by just watching.
3. It ain't over till it's over.
4. It's like déjà vu all over again.
5. No one goes there nowadays; it's too crowded.
6. Baseball is 90% mental and the other half is physical.
7. A nickel ain't worth a dime anymore.
8. Always go to other people's funerals; otherwise they won't come to yours.
9. We made too many wrong mistakes.
10. I knew the record would stand until it was broken.

My 1962 Yogi Berra baseball card is one of my prized possessions. I bought it at a yard sale in 1983 for 25 cents. I still remember the moment I discovered it in that shoebox under a bunch of "common" cards. I'm not exactly saying that this was the best moment of my life, better than when I exchanged wedding vows with my wife or when my kids were born... but I'm not exactly saying it wasn't either.

YOGI BERRA
Catcher-Outfield

New York
Yankees

DON MATTINGLY

*W*hy, oh why, would I focus on Don Mattingly, who will never be in the Hall of Fame, when there are so many other great Yankees from which to choose?

I am really glad you asked. The answer is simple, and maybe you can relate. Don "The Hit Man" Mattingly was my absolute favorite player growing up. I refused to miss a Mattingly at bat, ever. I even took a radio to the beach so I could listen to Yankee Hall-of-Famer Phil Rizzuto call the game while my sister buried her own toys (and, from time to time, our baby brother) in the sand. I would spend hours comparing Mattingly's stats to those of other players. I spent all of my summer paper route money, about $100, on a 1984 Mattingly rookie Donruss baseball card. (The card is now worth about $20. For some reason, I have also used the same "buy at the highest price possible" investment strategy with real estate and stocks.)

Do you have a favorite player? And do you think that, if you wrote a book about his team, you might feel kind of guilty if you didn't feature him? Yeah, that's just how I feel. I will not betray you, Donnie!

Don't get me wrong, Mattingly deserves plenty of accolades. For a span of a few years (1984-1986), he was totally dominant. He batted .343 in 1984, won the American League MVP with 145 RBIs in 1985, and racked up 238 hits in 1986. During this stretch, he actually had almost the same number of home runs as strikeouts! He set a record by hitting six grand slams in 1987.

There's one story I need to tell you about Don Mattingly. It was 1986, the baseball season was almost over, and Mattingly and future Hall-of-Famer Wade Boggs were vying for the American League batting title. In my mind, Boggs was the ultimate villain because he was a threat to Mattingly's claim to the batting title, plus he played for the hated Boston Red Sox and was a "slap hitter" with virtually no power. I would make a bet right now that you can hit the ball farther than Wade Boggs could.

But Boggs could hit for average, and he was leading the league in batting with a .357 average going into the season's final series with the Red Sox. Mattingly had a chance to catch Boggs and win the batting title. So what did Boggs do? He *claimed* he had an injury and sat out the entire series. This move meant that Mattingly would have to go 6 for 6 in the final game of the season to win the batting title. Mattingly went 2 for 5 with a homer, a double, and three RBIs, which was terrific but not enough to win the batting title.

Now, kids, violence is never the solution, and with that in mind I did not physically attack Wade Boggs when I saw him at the Museum of Natural History in New York City many years later. I did, however, give him the stink eye.

As a side note, I cried myself to sleep on December 16, 1992, the day Wade Boggs was traded from the Red Sox to the Yankees. I was 18 years old.

YANKEES

Topps®

DON
MATTINGLY OF-1B

MARIANO RIVERA

*F*inally, the 21st century!

Born in Panama, Mariano Rivera was a Yankee from 1995-2013 and spent most of his career as the team's closer. A thirteen-time All-Star and five-time World Series champion, Rivera is MLB's career leader in saves (652) and games finished (952). He was the first player ever to be elected unanimously to the Baseball Hall of Fame!

What made Rivera so good? It was his signature pitch: a sharp-moving, mid-90s-mile-per-hour cut fastball that frequently broke hitters' bats. Rivera was virtually unhittable in the postseason, with a 0.70 ERA.

As you can imagine, Mo was the most feared pitcher in baseball for many years. But he was also always humble and compassionate. He frequently gave to charities, he started his own charity after only three years in the major leagues, and in 2019 he was awarded the Presidential Medal of Freedom for all of the great things he has done to help people.

What an honor it would be to receive the Presidential Medal of Freedom. My guess is that someone has to nominate you. Could you do me this small favor, please? I am skeptical that e-mail or snail mail will make a strong enough impression, so please send your nominations to the White House by carrier pigeon. If I win, I'll mention you in my acceptance speech! If this seems like too much of a hassle, a favorable Amazon review will do just fine...

Anyway, Mariano Rivera's remarkable career proves that you don't have to be enormous or all muscle to be a great baseball player. Rivera was about 160 pounds when soaking wet... and wearing a backpack full of bricks.

The moral of the Rivera story is that you can do anything if you combine your skill with a strong will to do well and do good in the world. To be clear, the moral is not that you should fill your backpack with bricks, jump in the shower with your clothes on, and then weigh yourself.

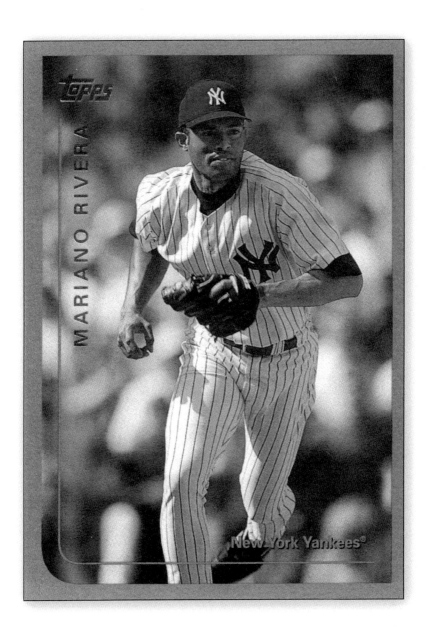

MARIANO RIVERA

New York Yankees®

DEREK JETER

*D*erek Jeter's stats during his 20-year career with the New York Yankees are incredible. He is the Yankees' all-time leader in hits (3,465), doubles (544), games played (2,747), stolen bases (358), times on base (4,716), and at bats (11,195). Jeter boasts five World Series rings and fourteen All-Star selections, and he was elected to the Baseball Hall of Fame in 2020 by a vote of 396 in favor and only one against. Do you know who voted against him? I don't either. If you find out, please let me know. The best way to contact me is by carrier pigeon. Feel free to use the same trusty pigeon that delivered your Presidential Medal of Freedom nomination to the White House.

What the statistics don't reflect is that Jeter conducted himself with real integrity during his entire career. He played hard, didn't complain, and was adored by fans.

I was at Jeter's final game at Yankee Stadium in 2014. Wouldn't you know it, he won the game with a single in his last at-bat! I was able to see this game because my friend Matt had tickets and he invited me to join him. I am friends with Matt for many reasons besides the fact that he gets great seats to incredible sporting events. That said, the Yankees are going to make the playoffs again soon, so if you are reading this, Matt... hint, hint.

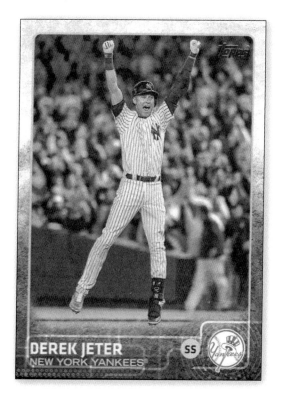

DEREK JETER
NEW YORK YANKEES

AARON JUDGE

*a*t 5 feet 4 inches, 141 pounds, Aaron Judge is the smallest active MLB player. Well, okay, maybe not. I'm just checking to see if you're paying attention to the numbers. Judge is actually a full fifteen inches taller and double that weight! Sorry, I couldn't let you get through this book without a little math.

More notably, Aaron Judge is a home run hitter. He hit a home run in his first at bat with the Yankees, on August 13, 2016. He also became the first rookie in MLB history to chalk up 45 home runs, 100 RBIs, and 100 runs. On August 27, 2019, he hit his 100th career home run, making him the third fastest MLB player to hit 100 home runs.

Home run hitters tend to strike out a lot. Aaron Judge strikes out a lot. I could provide you with some statistics, but I live in New York City and, if I run into Aaron Judge on the street, I would like it if he would simply pat me on the head. Did I mention that he is one giant dude?

I follow Aaron Judge on Twitter. While I realize he's probably got someone on hand to make sure he doesn't post anything stupid, he seems to be a friendly, kind person. I would also have an apple juice with Aaron Judge. (I would not, on the other hand, have an apple juice with Mickey Mantle. Although Mantle was an incredible baseball player, I'm afraid he would drink my apple juice while I'm not looking.)

Aaron Judge is likely to be a crucial part of the Yankees this season.

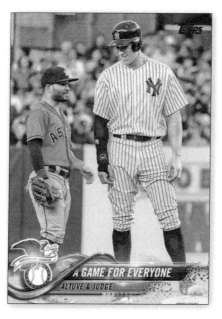

ONE UNBELIEVABLE YANKEES MOMENT

*W*hich moment do you think I have in mind? Babe Ruth calling his shot? Bucky Dent's 1978 home run, or maybe Aaron Boone's 2003 home run? Jeter's 2001 "flip"? There are so many incredible Yankees moments I could choose...

But I choose Scooter the Squirrel. During the 2007 baseball season, a squirrel decided to climb the right-field foul pole at old Yankee Stadium, some 200 feet tall. He kept coming back, too, and each time that squirrel appeared, the Yankees won the game! At some point, folks started calling him "Scooter" (the same nickname as the aforementioned Phil Rizzuto).

You don't believe it? Search online for "Yankee Stadium Squirrel" and see for yourself. We've just about reached the end of the book. And, yes, there may be someone telling you it's time to go to bed and under no circumstances are you allowed to look up another video. Never fear, this author has your back—consider trying any of these responses to delay bedtime:

"Don't worry, this is educational. Don't you value my education?"

"The author of the book I'm reading told me I had to. I understand your objection, but really your beef is with him, not with me. You can email him at dave@gmailemailhotmail.com."

"Okay, if you say so. My curiosity is burning, though, so can you please at least explain to me Einstein's theory of relativity instead? Just to be clear, I'd like to hear about both his general and special theories of relativity."

THE BEST YANKEES BASEBALL CARD EVER

*H*ere's my favorite Yankees baseball card. It's Oscar Gamble, sporting a tremendous 1970s Afro.

Made in the USA
Middletown, DE
11 July 2021

43960781R00022